MY
PONY BOOK

Written by
LOUISE PRITCHARD

DK PUBLISHING, INC.

DK

A DK PUBLISHING BOOK

Project Editor Anna McMurray
Project Art Editor Jamie Hanson
Senior Managing Editor Gillian Denton
Senior Managing Art Editor Julia Harris
Photographer Bob Langrish
DTP Designer Nicky Studdart
Production Lisa Moss
Picture Research Catherine Costelloe and Caroline Potts

First American Edition, 1998
2 4 6 8 10 9 7 5 3 1

Published in the United States by DK Publishing, Inc. New York, New York 10016

Library of Congress Cataloging-in-Publication Data
Pritchard, Louise
My pony book. – 1st American ed. / Written by Louise Pritchard.
    p. cm.
    Summary: Describes the characteristics, origins, and history of
ponies, from the powerful fjord to the minute, hardy Shetland, and
provides tips on their care and development.
    ISBN 0-7894-2810-5
    1. Ponies--Juvenile literature. [1. Ponies.] I. DK Publishing,
Inc.
SF315.M9 1998
636.1'6–DC21   97-34425 CIP   AC
Color reproduction by Colourscan, Singapore   Printed and bound in Italy by L.E.G.O.

Contents

WHAT IS A PONY?

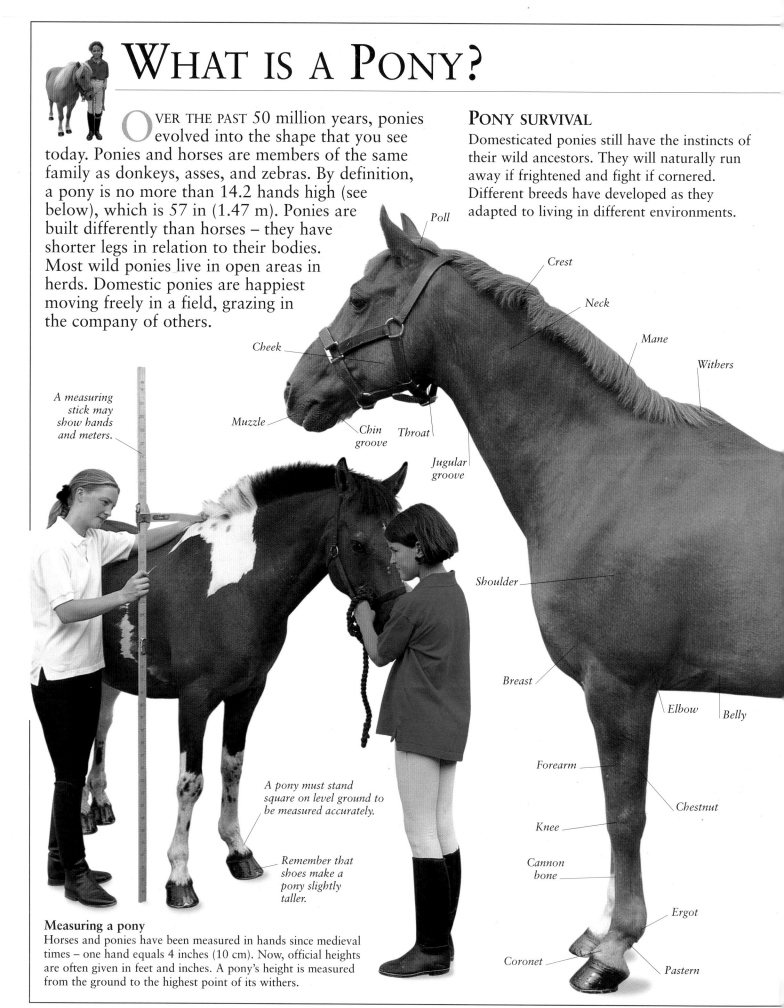

OVER THE PAST 50 million years, ponies evolved into the shape that you see today. Ponies and horses are members of the same family as donkeys, asses, and zebras. By definition, a pony is no more than 14.2 hands high (see below), which is 57 in (1.47 m). Ponies are built differently than horses – they have shorter legs in relation to their bodies. Most wild ponies live in open areas in herds. Domestic ponies are happiest moving freely in a field, grazing in the company of others.

PONY SURVIVAL

Domesticated ponies still have the instincts of their wild ancestors. They will naturally run away if frightened and fight if cornered. Different breeds have developed as they adapted to living in different environments.

A measuring stick may show hands and meters.

Poll

Crest

Cheek

Neck

Mane

Withers

Muzzle

Chin groove

Throat

Jugular groove

A pony must stand square on level ground to be measured accurately.

Shoulder

Breast

Elbow

Belly

Remember that shoes make a pony slightly taller.

Forearm

Chestnut

Knee

Cannon bone

Ergot

Measuring a pony
Horses and ponies have been measured in hands since medieval times – one hand equals 4 inches (10 cm). Now, official heights are often given in feet and inches. A pony's height is measured from the ground to the highest point of its withers.

Coronet

Pastern

8

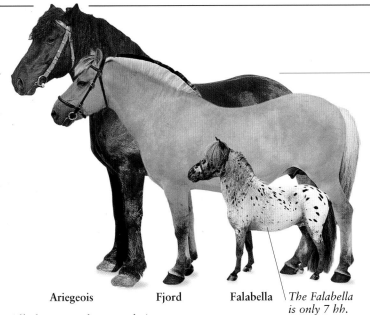

Ariegeois   Fjord   Falabella   *The Falabella is only 7 hh.*

All shapes, colors, and sizes

Ponies come in different shapes, colors, and sizes. Each breed has its own characteristics. Some, such as the Falabella, are classified as ponies because of their size – the Falabella is only 28 in (71 cm), but are actually thought to be horses because of their proportions.

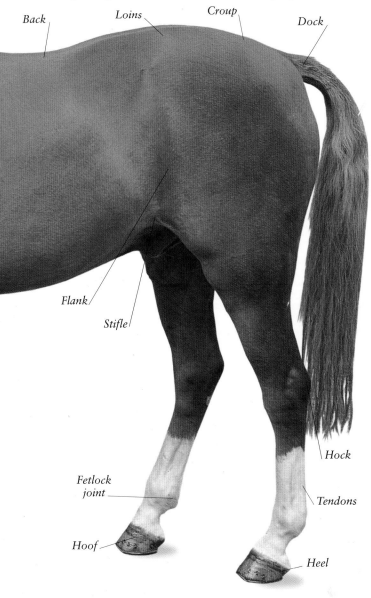

Back   *Loins*   *Croup*   *Dock*

Flank

Stifle

Hock

Fetlock joint

Tendons

Hoof

Heel

Hearing

Ponies have a very good sense of hearing. They can turn their ears to find out exactly where a sound is coming from. Ponies use their ears to pick up any sounds that may alert them to danger. **Ponies can hear things that humans cannot.**

Sight

A pony's eyes are set on the side of its head so it can see almost all around itself. However, it can see best in front of its face where the vision of both eyes overlaps.

Ponies have a blind spot of vision directly behind them.

Smell and taste

A pony uses its senses of smell and taste to decide whether something is good or bad to eat. It also uses its sense of smell to gain information about other ponies and identify them as friends or strangers.

Ponies love sweet and salty foods.

Tail

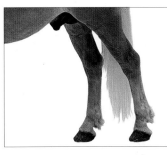

The tail is a good weapon for dislodging irritating flies. A swishing tail may mean a pony is angry; a clamped-down tail can mean a pony is cold or about to kick. A pony holds its tail high when it is excited.

The dock, located at the base of the tail, is made of bones and muscle.

Wild ponies

There are herds of wild ponies and horses in many countries around the world, such as these Dartmoor ponies from England. Some are truly wild, like the Przewalski; others are from domestic horses that have gone wild, like the Brumbies in Australia.

THE IDEAL PONY

A TRULY ideal pony will be healthy, have a friendly temperament, and enjoy its work. However, to a large extent, these attributes depend on a pony's human companions. No pony is perfect, but a pony that suits its owner should be considered ideal.

CONFORMATION

The shape of a pony and the way it is made is called its conformation. Ponies can be different shapes and sizes, but they must be correctly proportioned to carry themselves and a rider without strain or pain. A pony with good conformation will look good, move well, and be able to do the work that is asked of it.

Eyes should be set wide apart.

A long neck is elegant; a short neck indicates strength.

The chest should be wide enough to give space for the heart and lungs.

Ponies use their teeth to groom each other.

Teeth
Perfect teeth meet evenly at the front. If a pony's teeth do not meet, it cannot bite grass properly, although it can still chew. A wild pony would not survive if it could not bite off grass to eat. You can tell a pony's approximate age by its teeth because they change shape as the pony gets older.

Feet
A pony must have good feet if it is to stay healthy. Its feet should be symmetrical, so that an imaginary line drawn down the front of the leg divides the hoof exactly in half. Another imaginary line, drawn down the middle of the pastern, should be parallel to the front of the hoof.

The hind feet are slightly diamond shaped, whereas the front feet should be almost round.

Pastern

The hoof wall is made of the same material as human fingernails.

Underside of the foot
The soles of the feet should be hard and slightly concave to help the pony's feet grip the ground. Flat, spread feet are easily bruised. The rubbery structure in the middle of the foot is called the frog. It absorbs the impact of the foot hitting the ground, and helps prevent the pony from slipping.

Heels should be well apart.

Frog

Sole

Bar

Toe

Ideal for children
A Welsh Mountain Pony is a beautiful pony, known for being hardy and sound. It is one of several pony breeds that are suitable for children to ride, although most of the ponies ridden will be a mixture of breeds.

Withers should be higher than the croup.

Croup

The bones of the skull protect the brain.

The bones of the backbone are called the vertebrae.

A pony's skeleton

The skeleton consists of bones, cartilage, joints, and ligaments, which hold the joints together. A pony's conformation is based on its skeleton. Its shape depends on its breed. Ponies have eight pairs of "true" ribs that are attached to the breastbone and 10 pairs of "false" ribs that are attached to the breastbone by cartilage.

The ribs protect the heart and lungs.

The hock is the equivalent of your ankle.

The foot is the equivalent of your middle finger or toe.

Legs should be straight and symmetrical.

11

COLORS AND MARKINGS

THE COLORS and markings of a pony are used in its identification. On an official document, the shape and extent of markings are usually drawn on an outline of a pony. This is useful when the pony is sold, because a buyer can use it to check that the pony's identity is correct.

COLORING

Pigment gives a pony's skin, hair, or hoof wall its color. When there is no pigment, the coat grows white. Skin without pigment is very delicate and more likely to be damaged.

Wall eye

Face markings

A pony can have different white markings on its face. A star is a white marking between or above the eyes. A stripe is a vertical mark down the front of a pony's face. A wide stripe going down to the muzzle is often called a blaze.

Blaze   Star   Stripe

Brown eye

Eyes

Most ponies have brown eyes, but a few have one or two blue eyes, or white eyes, which have no pigment. These are called wall eyes.

Dorsal stripe

Leg markings

White leg marks come in all shapes and sizes. Some ponies may have only one leg with white on it, while other ponies have more.

White coronet   White sock

Hooves

A pony with a white sock or stocking is likely to have a pale-colored hoof, too. Some ponies have hooves that are mixed colors – part dark, part pale.

Pale horn   Dark horn   Every pony has its own unique markings.

Colors

The color of the body, mane, tail, legs, and skin determine a pony's official color. For example, a bay is reddish-brown, but has a black mane and tail, and black legs. A pony that has a white coat is known as a gray. All gray ponies have black skin. A pony with black, brown, and chestnut hair mixed with white is called a roan.

White and any color other than black (a piebald is black and white).

Skewbald

Reddish-brown, including the mane and tail.

Chestnut

Sandy to mouse-colored with black skin.

Dun

Golden with pale mane and tail.

Palomino

Gray with rings of darker gray.

Dapple gray

Some ponies are freeze-marked for security.

This pony is a bay.

13

IN THE WILD

THERE ARE FEW distinct species of wild horses or ponies. The Przewalski is probably the only really wild horse that still exists. It is the only survivor of four primitive types of horses that are thought to be the immediate ancestors of all modern horses and ponies. The others became extinct when they were hunted for food, or caught and domesticated more than 6,000 years ago.

Przewalski
This wild horse of Asia is a separate species within the family *Equidae*. It originally lived on the steppes of central Asia and Europe, but became extinct in the wild during the 1960s. It has recently been reintroduced to Mongolia from herds bred in captivity.

Short, chunky legs.

RUNNING WILD

There are horses and ponies running wild in many parts of the world. Some herds are descendants of domesticated animals and are described as feral. Others are only semiwild and are given food or brought in during harsh weather conditions.

Fjord pony
This attractive pony is native to Norway and was used by the Vikings more than 1,300 years ago. It is descended from the Przewalski, from which it has inherited strength.

Camargue horses are often called "the wild horses of the sea."

Mustangs

Herds of feral horses in North America are descended from horses introduced to America by the Spanish in the 16th century. The name mustang comes from the Spanish *mesteña*, which means a group of horses.

Exmoor ponies

Exmoor ponies are possibly the oldest British breeds, and live wild in the south of England. They have a thick mane and tail to protect them from the severe winter weather on the moors. They make excellent children's ponies.

Connemara ponies

This fast-moving pony is the only breed native to Ireland. The modern Connemara has a mixture of ancestors, including Arab, Welsh Cob, and Thoroughbred. It is a hardy pony that is able to survive in a harsh environment.

The Connemara is a superb jumper.

Camargue horses (left)

Herds of white horses have lived semiwild in the Camargue district of southern France for thousands of years. These strong, hardy horses survive on food they find in the reed beds of the Rhone delta.

Brumbies (above)

Herds of feral horses called Brumbies run wild in some remote parts of Australia. Their ancestors were introduced into Australia more than 200 years ago from South Africa and Europe.

GROWING UP

MARES COME into season (become fertile) every year between spring and autumn. After they mate with a stallion, they will have a single foal (it is very rare for a mare to have twins) about 11 months later. After the birth, the mother will clean the foal by licking it all over. While the foal is young, the mare is on constant guard against possible danger.

BIRTH

A new foal will be on its feet and suckling milk from its mother within one hour of birth. This milk contains antibodies, which help build up the foal's immunity to disease.

Pregnant Welsh Mountain Pony

Pregnant mares
A pony may not look pregnant, or in foal, until fairly late in her pregnancy. However, by the sixth month, the foal's movements can be seen, and the mare's belly is swollen.

A foal's mother, known as its dam, will get to know the smell and taste of her foal so she can identify it.

Mares in the wild

Mares in the wild usually give birth at night. The foals in a herd tend to stay together, and an adult will watch them. The foals soon learn the rules of behavior and hierarchy from their elders.

FOALS

A pony is not fully grown until it is at least five or six years old. By then, its bones are fully developed and strong, and it has a complete set of adult teeth. Between the ages of one and four years, a male foal is called a colt and a female foal is a filly. Young foals need a lot of rest and spend much time lying down.

A newborn foal has shaky legs. After five weeks, the bones have become stronger and the foal has an upright stance.

Two weeks
The foal has a short, bushy tail and stands with its back legs apart to aid stability.

Five weeks
The foal has a soft, woolly coat, known as milk hair. It is able to graze as well as suckle milk from its dam. The foal can be gradually weaned from its dam at six months.

Mares and their new foals need careful and gentle handling.

HUMAN TOUCH

Ponies are naturally curious, so a foal will want to find out about humans when it meets one. The dam will be protective of her young, so make sure the dam is comfortable with you before you touch or approach her foal.

When approaching mares and foals, try not to make any sudden movements.

A new foal should be gradually introduced to new things, such as wearing a halter and being handled.

A mare with her five-week-old foal

Eight weeks
The foal's body is becoming more muscular, and its milk hair is gradually being shed.

Four months
An adult coat is now in place. The neck has lengthened and the foal's tail has grown.

Five months
The foal's body has developed adult proportions. Its hooves have grown and hardened.

Natural Behavior

DOMESTIC PONIES have the same instincts and behavior patterns as their wild relatives. Although they have adapted well to living with humans, they can become stressed and unhappy if they are not given the freedom to behave naturally some of the time.

Personality

Watching ponies behaving naturally together in a field is a good way to learn about their personalities.

Ponies use a sensitive organ at the back of their nose, called the Jacobsen's organ, when they flehmen.

Scent detection

Ponies sometimes examine an unusual or interesting smell, such as a new type of feed, with the flehmen action. They take a deep sniff, then trap the air inside their nose by curling up their top lip to close off the nostrils.

Mutual grooming

Ponies that live outdoors should not be groomed with a body brush – they need the oil in their coats to keep them warm and dry. Ponies often groom each other with their front teeth to dislodge mud or to scratch an itch they can't reach themselves.

Mutual grooming is a way of making friends.

Rolling happily

Ponies often enjoy a good roll and may do so for many reasons. Domesticated ponies often roll after exercise or after a bath.

Some ponies can roll right over; others have to get up and down to roll on both sides.

Lazing around

Although ponies can sleep standing up, they lie down to get a deeper sleep – but only for about half an hour at a time. Foals often rest together on the ground while a mare keeps watch, alert for danger.

Living together

Ponies turned out together soon establish a hierarchy so that each one knows its place, but it is not necessarily the largest one that is dominant. When a new pony is introduced to a group, it should be allowed to meet the others one by one. Keep an eye on a new pony in a field to check that it is not being bullied by the other ponies. Some ponies will form a particular attachment and may not let other ponies talk to their friend.

Ponies can injure each other badly with a kick, especially when they are wearing shoes.

Fighting

Stallions in the wild will sometimes fight over mares, but will usually try to avoid injury by using threatening body language to win an argument. Domesticated ponies of both sexes may fight to keep their position within a group. Mares are often more aggressive than geldings.

Ponies may rear up to their full height and use their teeth and front legs to fight an opponent.

BODY LANGUAGE

A RIDER will build up a better relationship with a pony if he or she learn its language. A pony uses body language to show what it is thinking and how it feels. It will pick up on a rider's body language, too. Watch a pony carefully and learn to understand its signals.

COMMUNICATION

Ponies use all parts of their bodies to communicate their emotions. Some of their actions mean very different things from the same actions of other animals, such as dogs and cats.

Tell the pony firmly that it is not to kick, and be careful when you deal with its ticklish places.

Temperament
A rider needs to learn about a pony's temperament and how it will react in different circumstances.

Relaxed
Most ponies rest a hind leg when they are relaxed. Often a pony will rest one leg more than the other. Resting a front leg is not a good sign. It usually means there is something wrong.

The toe rests on the ground.

About to kick
If a pony doesn't like being groomed in certain places, it may lift a back leg to warn that it might kick if the grooming continues. This is also how it would warn another pony to keep away.

Horse whisperers
People who claim to be able to communicate with horses and ponies using their body language are often called horse whisperers. American Monty Roberts is well known for the way in which he can talk to horses.

Unhappy
The position of a pony's ears says a lot about what it is thinking. When the ears are laid back, the pony is angry or confused and frightened.

Listening
Ears that are moving backward and forward show that the pony is listening. It may do this when out riding as it "listens" to the rider's instructions.

Alert
A pony will prick its ears forward when it is alert and interested in something, such as the arrival of food. Take note if a pony does not look as interested as usual.

Cold weather
Most ponies will live happily outside all through the winter, because they grow a thick coat that keeps them warm. You will know if a pony is cold and unhappy. It will be standing on its own with its tail clamped down, uninterested in its surroundings.

Ears pricked forward show that life is fun at the moment.

Leg action of an excited pony may be higher than usual.

Showing off
When a pony is turned out in a field, it may show how excited it is by moving around with its tail and head held high. This is a way of showing off to any other ponies that may be watching. One way of stopping the pony from galloping around the field too much, and possibly injuring itself, is not to feed it before turning it out. If the pony is slightly hungry, it is more likely to eat grass instead of behaving too excitedly.

MISBEHAVIOR

A RIDER WILL NEVER win a battle of strength with a pony. If a pony is misbehaving, a rider should not lose his or her temper. Instead keep asking the pony kindly but firmly to do the right thing, and reward it when it does so. This requires a lot of understanding and patience, but it will be worth it in the end.

MISBEHAVING PONIES

You should work toward earning a pony's trust. There is really no such thing as a bad pony. In most cases of misbehavior, the pony is in pain, unhappy, or confused.

Will not walk on

If a pony stops suddenly, it may be frightened of something. Never give up when a pony will not walk on, but encourage it to move with persuasion, not anger.

Difficult to mount

If a pony will not stand still while you try to mount, or moves away from the mounting block, it may not understand what is expected of it. It could also mean the pony's saddle or back hurts, and it does not want any pressure on it.

Do not try to mount from too far away.

Hard to catch

If a pony is hard to catch, there is usually a reason why it doesn't want to come in or be ridden. A pony can be tempted with food, but make sure it has a nice time when it comes in so it will be easier to catch the next time.

Do not pull on the saddle when mounting.

To mount more easily, position the pony close to the mounting block and ask it to stand still.

Always eating

If a pony is allowed to get away with a bad habit, such as eating all the time, it will not know that this behavior is unacceptable. Ride the pony firmly past tempting food, so that it doesn't get a chance to put its head down.

Use your back and legs to keep the pony moving when it tries to eat.

Stable vices

Ideally, a pony should have at least two hours a day in a field or being ridden. Ponies that are stabled all the time may become bored and develop bad habits. These habits are often called stable vices and they can affect a pony's health. Crib-biting is when a pony holds on to a fixed object with its teeth, arches its neck, and sucks in air. When ponies gulp air it is called "wind-sucking."

Use kindness to teach a pony to behave as you would like it to, and the two of you will be friends.

OWNING A PONY

ANY PEOPLE dream of owning a pony, but underestimate what it involves. Although owning a pony is great fun and can be very rewarding, it also involves lots of hard work and expense. You are responsible for the pony's health and happiness. Many riding schools run camps where you can "own" a pony for a week and find out if you enjoy it.

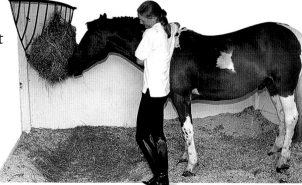

Companions
Ponies live in herds in the wild and will be lonely without the company of other ponies. If a pony lives alone, it will want your company instead. The more time you spend together, the better friends you will become.

WHAT YOU WILL NEED
If you are lucky enough to own a pony, you will need to buy lots of different equipment, which can be expensive. You should try to buy the best-quality equipment you can afford because it will last longer and be better for the pony.

A headcollar is used to tie up the pony.

Exercise
Riding is fun for both you and the pony. A pony will be happiest if you do a variety of activities, such as trail riding, taking a lesson, and sometimes schooling.

Most ponies enjoy going out for a ride, especially in the company of other ponies.

Riding clothes

Bridle

Saddle

First-aid kit

Grooming kit

Tack-cleaning equipment

There are many things a new owner will need to care for a pony properly.

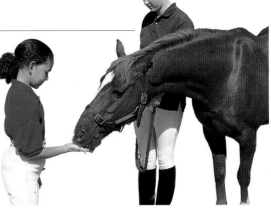

Meeting a pony
When you meet a pony for the first time you may want to give it a treat, such as an apple or carrot, but ask the owner first.

When you have a good ride on a pony, it makes all the hard work seem worthwhile.

Friends
Build up a good relationship with a pony, but never take it for granted. It will take a while for a pony to get used to you and the way you ride, just as it will take time for you to understand the pony.

Maintain contact with the pony so that it knows where you are.

Stable tools to keep the stable and stableyard clean.

A blanket keeps the pony warm in winter.

Straw is often used as bedding in the stable.

Leg wraps protect the pony's legs.

It is safer to approach a pony slowly, from the side, rather than from behind.

Wheelbarrow

Food such as pony nuts or coarse mix.

Correct handling
You must learn how to behave around a pony, and how to handle it. For example, if you want to pick up a pony's back foot, or brush its tail, keep in contact with the pony all the time, so that it knows where you are and what to expect.

Haynet

Feed bowls and buckets

The vet
A major expense when keeping a pony is the vet. However well you look after a pony, you will at some time need to call a vet. Put aside some money so that if there is an emergency, you will be able to pay for treatment. Even when a pony is completely healthy, it will need vaccinations against diseases such as tetanus and equine flu. This is particularly important if the pony is kept with other ponies, from which it might pick up infections.

A STABLEGIRL'S DAY

LOOKING AFTER A PONY is a responsible job and takes a lot of time. Domestic ponies rely on humans for their food and shelter, so it is important that they are looked after properly. There is much more to stable management than feeding a pony a few carrots and throwing on a saddle. Loving care will be rewarded by a pony's trust and a special relationship between pony and rider.

MORNING

If you are looking after a pony you will need to check it at least twice a day. Be prepared for hard work and an early start, especially during the school year when you have to fit the pony in with school. Ponies are much happier with a routine. A pony will soon learn to expect feeding, grooming, and exercise at roughly the same time every day.

Most ponies will enjoy time out in the field particularly with the company of other horses.

Taking the pony from the stable

Practice leading a pony from both sides.

Feeding
Ponies can become grouchy if kept waiting – particularly for food. A haynet morning and evening may be enough, but a working pony may need extra food such as pony nuts.

Cutting a hay bale

Turning out
Ponies that have been kept in a stable all night look forward to getting into the field for a good roll. A pony should always be turned out into a field with a plentiful water supply. During cold weather, check that the water is not frozen. A clipped pony should wear a blanket.

Separate droppings from the clean straw.

Mucking out
A stable must be kept clean and neat to keep a pony healthy. Every day, you will need to remove all the droppings and dirty straw and separate any clean straw so it can be used again in the evening. Leave the stable to air and let the floor dry before you lay down the bed again. Build up banks of bedding around the walls to help prevent the pony from becoming stuck when it lies down. Some people prefer wood shavings or shredded newspaper rather than straw for bedding, especially for ponies with respiratory problems.

You will need a wheelbarrow to carry droppings to the muck heap.

Checking the pony
As soon as you arrive at the stable, check that the pony is warm and well. Pick out its feet, and remove or replace any blankets so that the pony is comfortable. If the pony is staying in the stable for the day, it will need fresh water.

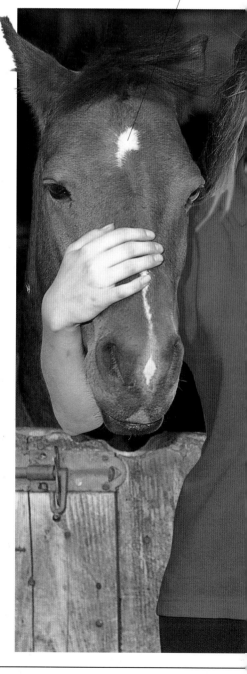

It is important to exercise stabled ponies daily.

AFTERNOON

Jobs such as taking care of tack can be done in the afternoon. This is also a good time to examine, exercise, and groom a pony. Grooming should be carried out daily to keep a pony's coat in good condition. It should be done soon after exercise, while the pony is still warm, because this makes it easier to get rid of the dirt. The more time you spend with a pony the better, because you will get to know the pony's moods and behavior.

Get a friend to help when you examine the pony.

Run your hand down the pony's leg to check for any signs of injury.

Daily care of a pony helps you develop a special bond.

Examination

If a pony has been in a field all day, it may be muddy. Carefully check it again for signs of illness or injury. All traces of mud need to be removed before the pony is tacked up, because a lump under the saddle or girth can rub and cause soreness.

Lunging a pony

Exercising a pony

If you do not have much time, or are unable to ride for any reason, lunging the pony for 20 minutes each day should be enough exercise for it. This should also be fun for both you and the pony.

Use saddle soap to clean the bridle.

Bedtime

After riding a pony, it is very important to clean the tack thoroughly. Clean tack is not only more comfortable for the pony to wear, it is also less likely to break if it is more supple. If a pony has been working hard, wash away the sweat marks. You may also need to put on a sweat blanket until the pony has cooled down. Make sure the straw is clean and dry in the pony's stable and that there is enough hay and fresh water to last until the following morning.

THE STABLE

IT IS NOT NATURAL for ponies to live in stables, but a pony may have to stay in, especially if the weather is very bad, or the pony is ill or injured. A stabled pony will need special care and attention from its owner if it is to stay as healthy and happy as possible.

THE IDEAL STABLE

A stable should be safe for a pony and large enough for it to turn around and lie down easily. Good ventilation is essential.

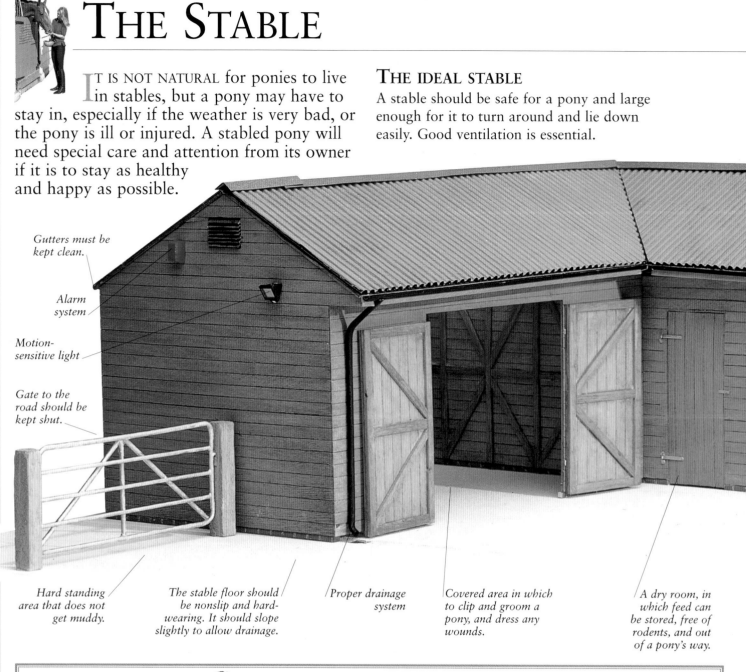

Gutters must be kept clean.

Alarm system

Motion-sensitive light

Gate to the road should be kept shut.

Hard standing area that does not get muddy.

The stable floor should be nonslip and hard-wearing. It should slope slightly to allow drainage.

Proper drainage system

Covered area in which to clip and groom a pony, and dress any wounds.

A dry room, in which feed can be stored, free of rodents, and out of a pony's way.

Mucking out

If possible, muck out a stable when the pony is not in it.

Try not to throw away any clean bedding.

Break up banks regularly.

The bed should be thick enough for you to drop the prongs of a fork on it without them hitting the floor.

1 Remove droppings
Remove the visible droppings, then separate the clean bedding from the dirty bedding.

2 Shovel dirty bedding
Shovel up the dirty bedding and tip it into a wheelbarrow. Most ponies will always wet the floor in the same place.

3 Replace bedding
Throw clean bedding up against the wall so that any loose droppings fall down. Sweep them up with any remaining dirty bedding.

4 Flatten bedding
Put back the bedding as level as possible. Flatten banks around the walls with the back of the fork.

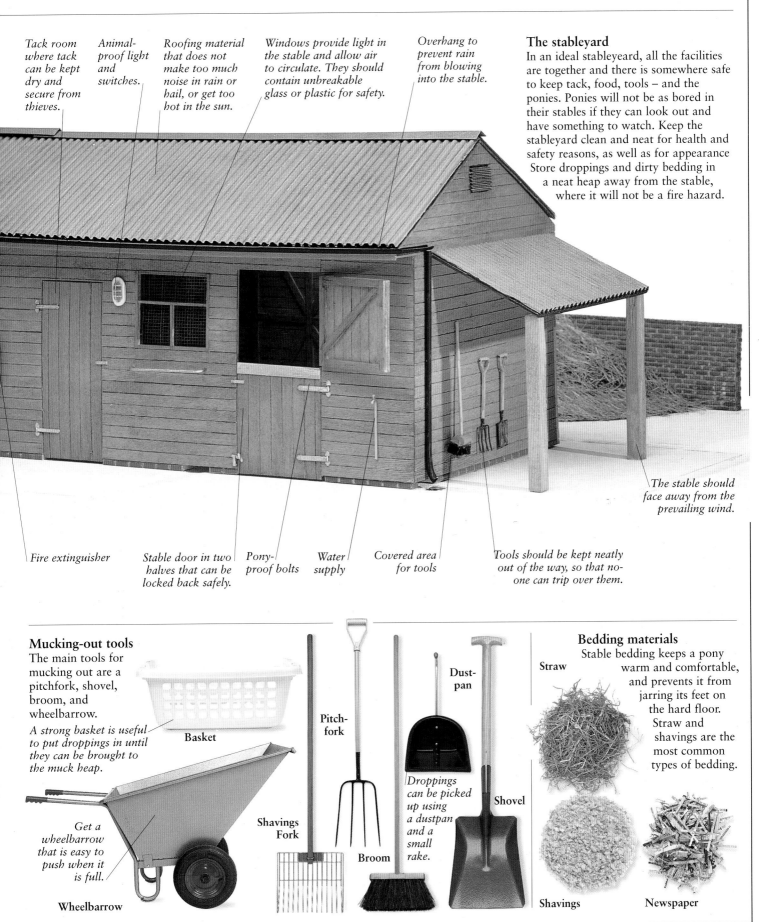

Tack room where tack can be kept dry and secure from thieves.

Animal-proof light and switches.

Roofing material that does not make too much noise in rain or hail, or get too hot in the sun.

Windows provide light in the stable and allow air to circulate. They should contain unbreakable glass or plastic for safety.

Overhang to prevent rain from blowing into the stable.

The stableyard

In an ideal stableyeard, all the facilities are together and there is somewhere safe to keep tack, food, tools – and the ponies. Ponies will not be as bored in their stables if they can look out and have something to watch. Keep the stableyard clean and neat for health and safety reasons, as well as for appearance Store droppings and dirty bedding in a neat heap away from the stable, where it will not be a fire hazard.

The stable should face away from the prevailing wind.

Fire extinguisher

Stable door in two halves that can be locked back safely.

Pony-proof bolts

Water supply

Covered area for tools

Tools should be kept neatly out of the way, so that no-one can trip over them.

Mucking-out tools

The main tools for mucking out are a pitchfork, shovel, broom, and wheelbarrow.

A strong basket is useful to put droppings in until they can be brought to the muck heap.

Basket

Get a wheelbarrow that is easy to push when it is full.

Wheelbarrow

Pitch-fork

Shavings Fork

Dust-pan

Droppings can be picked up using a dustpan and a small rake.

Broom

Shovel

Bedding materials

Stable bedding keeps a pony warm and comfortable, and prevents it from jarring its feet on the hard floor. Straw and shavings are the most common types of bedding.

Straw

Shavings

Newspaper

THE FIELD

PONIES LOVE to be turned out in a field where they can graze, exercise themselves, and, if possible, enjoy the company of other ponies. Most ponies can tolerate both hot and freezing conditions, so they can live outside all year round if they are properly fed and looked after.

Fresh water
Ponies need to have permanent access to fresh water. They drink more in dry weather, or when their main diet is dry food, such as hay, rather than moist grass.

A water trough should be large enough for several ponies to drink from at once.

IDEAL FIELD
A field must be large enough for the number of ponies that live there. One pony living out all the time needs about 1.5 acres (0.6 hectares). The field should be flat, well-drained, easy to get to, and contain grass that is nutritious, but not too rich.

Cleaning
Ponies have to be wormed regularly, but worms can easily be picked up again if a field has not been managed properly. Droppings have to be picked up at least once a week, because this is where the worm eggs live.

Fencing
One of the best types of fencing for ponies is a post-and-rail fence, but like any fence, it must be kept in good repair.

Some ponies chew fences so the wood should be painted with an unpalatable, nontoxic substance.

Shelter
Ponies that live in a field need shelter from the weather. A large tree can offer protection from the sun. A thick hedge or wall around the field provides shelter in winter.

Barbed wire

Although barbed wire is cheap and effective fencing, it can be dangerous for ponies. If it becomes loose and tangled, ponies can get their legs trapped and sustain serious injuries.

Barbed wire must not be used near the ground where ponies can get their feet caught.

Garbage

All garbage must be removed from a field before ponies can be turned out, because they may try to play with it and injure themselves. Rusty metal is especially dangerous.

Dangerous water

If there is a stagnant pond or water that is polluted in a field, it must be fenced off so that the ponies can't get to it. If a pony drinks polluted water, it could become ill. Any marshy ground near water is also dangerous because a pony could become stuck it.

Poisonous plants

There are several plants that are poisonous to ponies and can cause them serious illness, or even kill them. These plants are still poisonous when they are dried, and even more dangerous, because the ponies are more likely to eat them. If there are poisonous plants in a field they should be dug up and burned.

Yew

All parts of the yew tree are poisonous, and unfortunately, many ponies seem to like eating it. Even a small amount can be fatal and its effects can be very sudden.

Oak

Acorns and oak leaves are poisonous. A pony that eats a large amount of acorns can become ill from constipation or kidney damage.

FEEDING

A PONY'S NATURAL food is grass and herbs. It has a small stomach and is designed to eat little and often. Roughage, such as hay, should be the main part of a pony's diet. The daily ration should be given in portions, so that the pony has food to eat throughout the day and night.

THE RIGHT AMOUNT

The amount of food a pony should be fed will vary according to the amount of work it is doing. Most ponies get enough nutrition from grass and hay to maintain their condition. A pony doing even small amounts of work may need extra food to give it energy.

Filling and tying a haynet

1 Hold the net open with one hand and pack the hay in. Be careful the drawstring doesn't become tangled up with the hay.

You can leave the hay in slices or shaken up.

2 When the right amount is in the haynet, tie it to the stable wall, or to a fence or tree in a field, so that it is at the pony's eye level.

If the net is tied too high, dust and seeds may fall in the pony's eyes.

3 Thread the string through the bottom of the net and pull it up. In this way, when the net is empty, it will not hang down where the pony can catch its foot in it.

Pull the net up as high as possible.

4 Tie the string with a quick-release knot and turn the knot away from the pony to make sure it does not accidentally undo it when eating.

Thread the loose end of the haynet through the net.

For a pony to stay healthy, its natural eating habits must be maintained.

Stabled ponies in particular need something succulent, such as apples, in their diet, to make up for the lack of grass.

Ponies need clean, good-quality food.

Types of food

Cereals such as treated oats and barley provide energy in quantities small enough for a pony's digestive system to cope with. Roughage such as chaff, which is chopped straw, mixed in with food will help stop a pony from eating too quickly.

Pre-mixed food, such as coarse mixes and nuts or cubes, provide a balanced diet with the right vitamins and minerals.

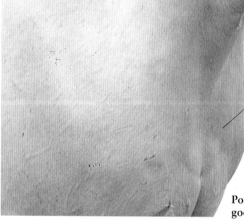

Corn

Barley

Bran

Coarse mix

When feeding a pony, keep your hand flat and your thumb out to the side so that the pony does not bite your fingers by mistake.

Drinking water
A pony needs fresh water available at all times. If there is a bucket of water in the stable, it must be changed twice a day.

Give two or more small quantities of concentrates at the same time each day.

Weighing food
It is essential to weigh food carefully before you give it to a pony. Never guess how much food you are giving a pony because you may not be feeding it the right amount it needs to stay healthy.

Chaff

Cooked linseed

Oats

Apple
Carrot
Turnip
Fruit and vegetables

Salt lick

Individual needs
Although there are basic rules of feeding, each pony is an individual with its own needs. The amount of food one pony needs to eat to stay healthy may be different than that of other ponies.

HEALTH

THE MAIN SIGNS of good health are a shiny, sleek coat, loose, supple skin, bright eyes, a well-covered body, and a good appetite. A healthy pony is one that is fit and able to work. It should stand and behave normally, digest its food properly, and be alert and interested in its surroundings. Each day, a rider should check for signs of injury by running a hand all over the body and legs, keeping an eye out for swellings, cuts, or pain. He or she must also learn what is normal for a pony they are looking after, so they will know immediately if something is wrong.

Food and water

Feeding and watering a pony is essential for good health. Ponies should also be wormed regularly so that they, and not the worms, get the food. Their teeth should also be checked every six months to remove any sharp edges or deal with other problems.

SYMPTOMS

At rest, a pony should be happy to stand on all four feet, although most ponies rest a hind leg. Legs should not be swollen or hot to the touch. Temperature, respiration, and pulse should be normal.

It is important to learn to recognize signs of injury or illness.

The pony should take strides of equal length.

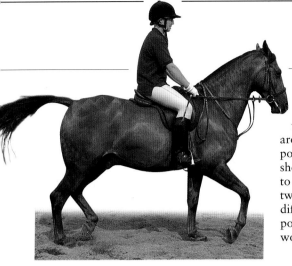

Regular exercise gradually builds up a pony's fitness.

Plenty of exercise

Ponies in the field exercise themselves as they walk around looking for food. A pony that lives in a stable should, ideally, be taken out to stretch its legs for at least two hours every day. Work is different than exercise, and a pony must not be asked to work hard until it is fit.

Staying warm

In winter, a pony may need to wear a blanket to keep it warm and dry, especially if its coat has been clipped. If a pony is allowed to get cold and wet, it will be miserable and lose condition because too much energy from its food is being used to produce body heat. Some unclipped ponies may be kept warm enough by their own natural winter coat.

The membranes under the eyelids and in the nostrils should be a salmon-pink color.

A healthy pony will eat well and chew normally.

A foal should be up and running with its mother within a few hours of being born.

Pick out hooves

Even when a pony is living out in the field, its hooves need to be picked out and checked every day. If a pony's feet are not looked after, it may go lame.

Frog

Use a hoof pick toward the toe.

A blanket should fit properly so that it is comfortable for the pony to wear.

First-aid kit

It is important to have a basic first-aid kit handy to treat any minor wounds and injuries. The vet must be called to treat serious illness or injury.

Gamgee bandage

Scissors

Bandage   **Cold treatment pack**   **Antiseptic liquid and spray**

The farrier

A farrier looks after a pony's shoes and feet. Shoes protect the hoof from being worn away by the rough surfaces of roads and paths. A farrier needs to trim the pony's feet about every five or six weeks, because the pony's hooves grow all the time.

CARING FOR A PONY

GROOMING KEEPS a pony clean, helps its circulation, and removes parasites that feed on dead hair and skin. Ponies like being groomed and it also gives a rider an opportunity to check the pony over. The best time to groom is after exercise, when the skin is warm and the pony is relaxed. A full groom of a stabled pony is called strapping, and it should take about 45 minutes.

A hoof pick should have a blunt end so that it does not accidentally puncture the pony's foot.

GROOMING KIT

Every pony should have their own grooming kit. This lessens the risk of passing disease from one pony to another. A plastic tray, labeled with the pony's name, is ideal for keeping everything in. Wash the brushes and curry combs occasionally, otherwise you will brush dirt onto the pony, rather than off it.

Cleaning feet
Pick out the pony's feet into a skip. The hoof pick should be used from heel to toe so it cannot jab into the pony's leg by mistake. Pull it down both sides of the frog and check each foot carefully for any wounds.

Squeeze most of the excess water out of the sponge, so that you don't get water in the pony's eyes.

Sponging the muzzle
The grooming kit should contain two sponges – one for the eyes, nose, and mouth, and one for the dock. Wash the eyes with a damp sponge to clean the eyelids. Use a damp sponge to clean the pony's nostrils and lips, too.

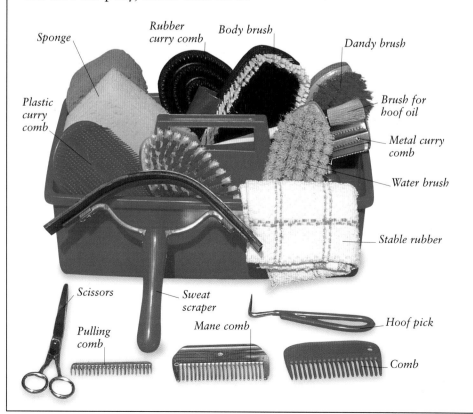

Sponge

Rubber curry comb

Body brush

Dandy brush

Plastic curry comb

Brush for hoof oil

Metal curry comb

Water brush

Stable rubber

Scissors

Sweat scraper

Mane comb

Hoof pick

Pulling comb

Comb

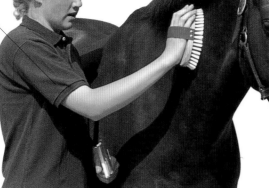

Use the right hand on the pony's off-side and the left hand on the nearside.

Brushing the body

Use a rubber curry comb or dandy brush to remove dried mud from the pony's body. Never use a metal curry comb. If the pony is stabled most of the time, use the body brush all over its body and legs, starting with the neck. Brush hard to bring the loose hair, grease, and dirt to the surface. Do a final polish with the curry comb. Brush the face gently with a soft brush.

Bring the mane back to the right side of the neck and use fingers and a body brush to remove any tangles.

Brushing the mane

The mane is groomed after the pony's crest. The mane can be made to lie flat by "laying" it (brushing it with a damp water brush) once the rest of the grooming is finished.

Clean the brush with a metal curry comb after every four or five strokes.

Never use a dandy brush or curry comb on the tail.

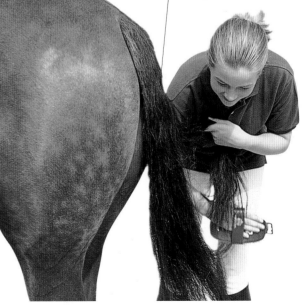

Brushing the tail

Stand to one side of the pony to brush its tail. Hold the tail in one hand and gradually let the hairs down until you have brushed the whole tail. Use your fingers and a body brush to untangle any knots.

GROOMING FOR A SHOW

GETTING READY for a show is great fun, but it does take a lot of time to do properly, so a rider needs to be prepared. Even if rider and pony do not win any rosettes, it is thoroughly rewarding to make a pony look its best on a special occasion.

ASK FOR HELP

It takes practice to make a pony look really sharp for a show. You may like to ask a more experienced person to help you at first, especially with braiding.

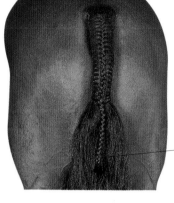

Braiding the tail

To braid a pony's tail, start with a small group of hairs from each side of the dock, and from the center of the tail. Gradually join more groups of hair from the sides, until the tail is braided to the bottom of the dock. Continue the braid to the bottom of the tail, without joining more hairs, then loop the braid under and secure it with a thread.

A well-braided tail makes a pony look very neat.

Use hairspray to tame any strands that escape from a braid.

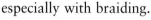

Don't leave a tail bandage on for more than an hour.

Undo the braid when it is dry, and brush out the tail to make it look fuller than usual.

Thickening the tail

After washing a pony's tail, put on a tail bandage down to the bottom of the dock. To make the tail look thicker than it really is, divide it into three sections and make one large braid while it is still wet.

Oiling the hooves

Hoof oil comes in black or clear. Although it does not improve the horn, you can brush it on when you want to make a pony look extra sharp.

Make sure the hooves are clean before you brush on oil.

Trim any feathers at the back of the legs.

Oiling the hooves

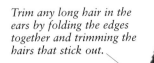

Trim any long hair in the ears by folding the edges together and trimming the hairs that stick out.

Braiding the mane

1 Dampen the mane with a water brush and divide it into equal bunches with a mane comb. Use elastic bands to keep the bunches separate.

Wash the mane the day before the show, or it will be too slippery to braid.

2 Start braiding near the poll. As you complete the braid, turn under the ends and thoroughly secure them with a thread.

Sew through the end, wind the thread around, and sew back through the end.

3 Push the needle through the top of the braid from underneath, to fold the braid under. Pull the thread tight, then fold the braid in half again.

Use thread the same color as the pony's mane.

4 Wind the thread around the braid several times, and sew backwards and forwards to secure it. Cut the ends of the thread close to the braid.

The finished braid should be short, neat, and close to the crest of the pony's neck.

5 Depending on its size, a pony will have seven or nine braids. Traditionally, there should always be an odd number of braids.

Lots of braids make a short neck look longer; fewer, larger braids make a long neck look shorter.

Rub a small amount of baby oil over the pony's muzzle to keep the muzzle in good condition.

Practice braiding before you actually need to do it for a show.

Braiding the forelock
Make one braid from the forelock. Braid it in exactly the same way as the rest of the mane. When it is finished, it should sit in the middle, between the ears. Be careful not to get the needle in the pony's eyes if it moves suddenly.

Fold the braid under twice to make a neat "ball" of hair.

RIDING CLOTHES

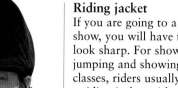

THERE are lots of formal and fun riding clothes for young riders. If you are just starting to ride, there is no need to buy expensive new clothes. Instead, wear something that is safe, comfortable, and warm in winter. Before your first lesson, ask the riding school what they recommend.

EVERYDAY CLOTHES

For everyday riding, casual clothes are fine. However, a hat that fits correctly, and conforms to the latest safety standards is vital. In many countries, it is illegal not to wear one. If you are able to ride regularly, you may decide to get special riding clothes.

Jodhpurs or breeches are best because they stretch and have no uncomfortable seams in the wrong place. Breeches are only calf-length, so they are worn with long boots.

Boots should have a low heel and a smooth sole.

Riding jacket
If you are going to a show, you will have to look sharp. For show-jumping and showing classes, riders usually wear a riding jacket with a white shirt and tie, and pale-colored jodhpurs or breeches.

Riding jackets are popular for shows.

Jodhpurs and breeches have an extra layer of material on the inside of the leg.

Boots come in different lengths and widths.

The chin-strap on the hat must be adjusted correctly to fit.

Gloves protect hands and provide extra grip on the reins.

Dressage outfit

For dressage classes, you may be expected to wear a sharp black or navy-blue jacket with a white shirt. Check with the organizers of the show before you arrive, so that you are wearing the right outfit, and don't have to worry about anything except the test. A black or navy-blue velvet hat looks good when it matches a rider's jacket. If you are wearing a skull cap, make sure the silk fits the cap properly.

Use a stock pin to do up the stock.

Gloves and breeches should be the same color.

Cream or white breeches look smart.

Make sure that boots are clean.

This crash helmet has silk on it.

Matching shirt and silks worn for cross-country.

A body protector in case a rider falls.

Cross-country outfit

Schooling whip

A riding whip is for everyday riding and jumping.

Wool gloves

String gloves

Riding gloves have grip on the palms.

Riding whip

Jodhpur boots

Formal wear

In advanced dressage competitions, riders are expected to wear formal clothes. The black or navy-blue jacket has tails and the "points" of a waistcoat attached in the front. These "points" come in different colors. Some riders may wear a separate jacket and waistcoat. Top dressage riders wear a top hat, rather than a crash helmet. White jodhpurs, long leather boots, a white stock, and white gloves complete the outfit.

TACK

THE MAIN ITEMS of tack are the saddle and the bridle. They are designed to help a rider control a pony and to make the ride more comfortable for both. Tack should be looked after carefully. It is expensive to replace, and if allowed to become hard and cracked, it will be uncomfortable for the pony. It could even break during riding and cause an accident. Tack should last for years if you clean it regularly and store it properly.

SADDLES AND BRIDLES

There are three main types of saddles. Jumping and dressage saddles are designed to help the rider in these particular disciplines. A general-purpose saddle is for non-specialists, and is the type used by most riders. The two main types of bridle are a snaffle, which has a single rein, and a double bridle, which has two bits and two sets of reins.

Saddle

Most saddles are made of leather, although other materials can be used. They are built around a framework called a "tree." Trees were traditionally made of wood, but many are now made of fiberglass.

Gullet

Saddle flap

Girth straps

Panel

Underside of general-purpose saddle

Cantle

Seat

Pommel

Stirrup leather and iron

Girth

Saddle flap   **Dressage saddle**

Cantle   *Seat*   *Horn*

Flank girth billet

Fender

Stirrup   *Cinch*

Western saddle

For the western style of riding, riders have special western saddles. The saddles are deep, with long stirrup leathers to give a comfortable ride. They were originally designed for cowboys and girls in the United States, who need to spend many hours in the saddle rounding up and driving cattle. Western saddles are heavier than saddles used for the English style of riding because they have to withstand rough treatment.

Cleaning the saddle

Remove grease and mud with a damp cloth, then use a sponge to rub in saddlesoap over the saddle. Treat a saddle with oil occasionally, especially if it is new.

Cleaning the bridle

Clean the bridle every day in the same way as the saddle. Remove grease and mud first, then rub saddlesoap into all the different pieces. Once a week, take the bridle apart and clean it more thoroughly, checking all the stitching as you do so. Make sure you learn how to put it back together again properly.

Bit

Bridle

There are many different types of bit and several types of noseband to give a rider more control. A simple snaffle bridle is usually the best type to use on a pony. Ask your instructor for advice and use a bridle which suits the pony best.

Cavesson noseband

Throatlash fastens on the near side.

Bit must fit so that it lies over the horse's tongue without pinching.

Tack-cleaning equipment

To clean tack properly, you will need a damp cloth or sponge to remove dirt, saddlesoap and a sponge, leather oil or other dressing and a brush, metal polish, and a cloth (not to be used on the mouthpiece of the bit), a duster for polishing metal, a stiff brush for non-leather tack, and a tack cover or other cloth to place over the clean saddle.

Duster

Tack cover

Damp cloth

Dry cloth

Sponge

Stiff brush

Brush for oil

Saddle-soap

Metal polish

Leather oil

Storing tack

Tack should be stored somewhere dry. Place the saddle on a proper support, never on a narrow support, such as the back of a chair. Hang the bridle from the headpiece.

TACKING UP

ONE OF THE most important things about tacking up is that the tack fits correctly. Ill-fitting tack can bruise and hurt the pony. If a rider is unsure, they should ask an instructor or a tack expert to check the fit. After riding, the saddle should be removed immediately. Ponies like rolling after a ride and may do so even with the saddle on, which could not only damage the saddle, but also hurt the pony's back.

PUTTING ON A SADDLE

Before you put on the saddle, remove any mud or stable stains from the pony's coat. Dirt left under the saddle or girth will rub the pony and be painful. Use a saddle pad or sheepskin under the saddle. This not only keeps the saddle clean, but also makes it more comfortable for the pony.

Keep the pony tied up while you put on its saddle.

1 The saddle cloth
Place the saddle cloth over the pony's withers. It should be slightly too far forward at first.

3 Placing the saddle
Slide the saddle cloth and saddle back together into the proper position on the pony's back. Pull the saddle cloth up into the arch and gullet of the saddle at the same time, so that it is not tight across the pony's back.

4 Lower the girth
Go around the other side of the pony to check that the saddle flaps are lying flat, and that the saddle cloth is not caught up. Fix on the girth or pull it down if it is already attached to the saddle. Come back to the nearside of the pony and lift the girth up under its belly.

Pull the buckle guards down on both sides.

5 Buckle up the girth
Fix the girth to the same straps on both sides. For safety, always use the front strap and one other because they are attached to different parts of the saddle. To take off the saddle, run up the stirrups, undo the girth, and lift the saddle off towards you.

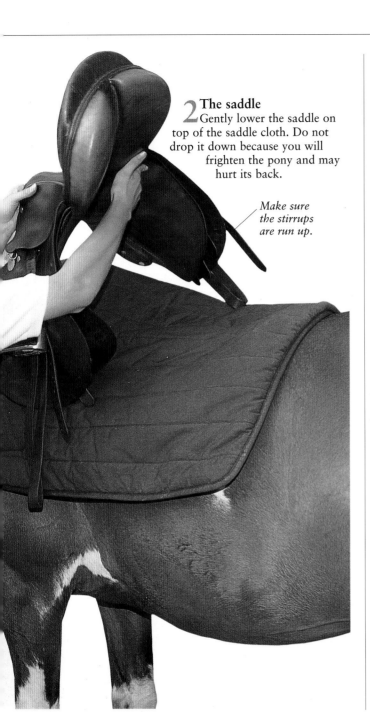

2 The saddle
Gently lower the saddle on top of the saddle cloth. Do not drop it down because you will frighten the pony and may hurt its back.

Make sure the stirrups are run up.

BRIDLES
Before you start to put the bridle on, check that it is not tangled. Stand on the pony's left and behave gently and calmly. To take off the bridle, undo the throatlash and noseband, then pull the reins and headpiece together over the pony's ears.

1 The reins
Place the reins over the pony's head before its headcollar is removed. This means that you will always have some control over the pony, and be able to stop it from walking away. Never let it escape with its bridle half on.

2 The bit
Hold the bridle in front of the pony's face with your right hand. Use your left hand to place the bit in the pony's mouth. Ask the pony to open its mouth by pressing your thumb gently on the gum in the gap in its teeth.

3 The headpiece
Bring the headpiece over the pony's ears one by one. Pull the forelock over the browband, and check that everything is lying straight.

4 The throatlash
Do up the throatlash first, because this keeps the bridle on. You should be able to fit your whole hand between the pony's head and the throatlash when it is done up.

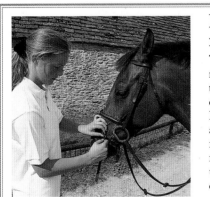

Flash noseband
This is a drop noseband attached to a loop in the cavesson noseband. It goes below the bit, and prevents a pony from opening its mouth too wide. Do it up tighter than a plain cavesson noseband.

5 The noseband
Fasten the noseband. An ordinary cavesson noseband goes under the cheek pieces and above the bit. It should be done up loosely so that two fingers can just fit underneath the noseband.

LEARNING TO MOUNT

MOUNTING IS one of the first things to learn about riding. It is usual to mount from the ground, but a mounting block or leg-up may make it easier. A rider will normally mount from the left of the pony, but ideally, should be able to mount from either side, in case of an emergency.

MOUNTING

Before mounting, you should introduce yourself to the pony, and check that the tack is done up properly. Try not to be too nervous because the pony will sense your mood.

Hold on to the reins to control the pony while mounting.

2 Foot in the stirrup
Put your left foot in the stirrup. Turn to face the pony's side. Place your right hand on the saddle, but do not hold on to it.

Be careful not to poke your foot into the pony.

Stand close to the pony's shoulder.

1 Prepare to mount
Check that the stirrups are down, and tighten the girth to prevent the saddle from slipping as you mount. Stand at the pony's left shoulder, facing the tail. Hold the reins on the pony's withers in your left hand. Turn the stirrup toward you with your right hand.

The stirrup position
To prevent the stirrup leather from being twisted as you mount, turn the back of it toward you.

Try not to kick the pony in the back as your right leg swings over.

The pony should not move off until you ask it to do so.

Sit straight in the saddle.

Try to make the pony stand still while you mount.

Keep the toes pointing forward and the heels down.

3 Into the saddle
Push off from the ground with your right foot. Stand with your weight on your left foot, which is in the stirrup. Swing your right leg over the pony's back. Never pull yourself up by the saddle because this can damage the saddle, and is also bad for the pony.

4 Sit straight
Lower yourself gently into the saddle and put your right foot into the stirrup, so that the ball of your foot rests on the iron. Take up the reins evenly in both hands and settle into your seat. Both you and the pony are now ready to walk forward.

Dismounting

Let your right hand rest on the saddle.

Don't pull on the saddle as you dismount.

1 Getting off
You should dismount from the near side. Put the reins in your left hand and take both feet out of the stirrups. Lean forward and swing your right leg over the pony's back.

2 Sliding down
Dismount slowly and calmly, holding the reins to keep the pony still. As you lower yourself to the ground at the pony's side, avoid tugging at the reins.

3 Landing
Keep your knees bent as you land. After you have dismounted, shorten both stirrups and remove the tack. Remember to thank the pony.

RIDING

A PONY MOVES in four main ways, called gaits. At whatever speed a pony is traveling, a rider will need to tell it when to stop, turn, or go faster. This is done using signals called aids. Natural aids are the hands, legs, seat, and voice.

LEARNING THE AIDS

Learning the natural aids is like learning a new language. A good rider can make a pony do whatever they want, without appearing to move their body.

A pony can interpret more easily what aids are being given if the rider is balanced and comfortable in the saddle.

A well-trained pony will already understand the aids.

The pony should stand square, with its weight evenly distributed among all four feet.

Stopping
When you want to stop, squeeze the reins and sit tall in the saddle. Pull gently on the reins if necessary, but stop pulling the moment the pony halts.

Always look where you are going. As you transfer your weight, the pony will know which way to go.

Starting to move
Ask the pony to walk in a straight line by squeezing its sides equally with both legs. Hold your hands level above the pony's withers, a few inches apart, so that you can just feel its mouth.

Holding the reins
Pass the reins between the fourth and pinky fingers. Hold them between the thumb and first finger, with the thumb on top. Let the loop of the reins hang down toward the pony's left shoulder.

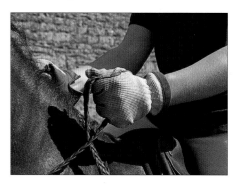

Turning
Squeeze the inside rein. When turning left, this is the left rein because it is on the inside of the turn. Hold the inside leg on the girth to keep the pony from moving forward. The outside leg is held just behind the girth to stop the pony from swinging out its hindquarters.

Let the outside hand move forward as the pony turns.

Wrists are supple and straight.

Walking
The pony moves each foot in turn – one hindfoot, then the forefoot on the same side, then the other hindfoot, then the second forefoot.

Trotting
Trotting is faster and bumpier than walking. It is a two-time pace. The pony moves diagonally opposite feet together. You can sit to the trot, but it is more comfortable to rise up and down in the saddle with the pony's movement.

In a rising trot, a rider moves up and down, in time with the trot.

Cantering
Normally, cantering is faster than a trot. However, when a pony is being schooled, cantering can be slower. The canter is a three-time gait and can be very comfortable to ride. The pony moves one hindfoot, then the other hindfoot and opposite forefoot together, then the second forefoot.

Sit deep in the saddle.

Galloping
The gallop is a four-time gait. The pony moves its feet in the same order as the canter, but the hindfoot of the diagonal pair goes down just before the forefoot. A pony should not be made to gallop until it is fit enough and you know that you can stop it.

When you gallop, lean forward out of the saddle slightly.

JUMPING

ONCE A RIDER is balanced and able to control a pony, they are ready to learn how to jump. Jumping is great fun and requires confidence from both rider and pony. Balance, rhythm, and impulsion are the keys to a good approach. Balance means that the rider's weight is well distributed, rhythm is when the pace is steady and constant, and impulsion means that the pony is moving forward, willingly and with energy. An inexperienced rider should learn to jump on an experienced pony.

HOW A PONY JUMPS

There are five stages in a jump – the approach, takeoff, moment in midair, landing, and get-away. It is important to concentrate through all the stages so that you and the pony clear the jump well, and are ready to approach the next fence.

Fold forward at the hips and look ahead between the pony's ears.

The pony should take off about the same distance away from the jump as the height of the jump.

Keep your weight down in your heels.

Over-reach boots protect the pony's heels in case it treads on them with its back feet.

A pony takes off from both hind feet.

Let the pony find its own way through the poles.

The distance between the poles should suit the pony's stride.

Trotting poles

At the beginning of a jumping lesson, an instructor will probably lay some poles on the ground for the pony to trot over. This exercise makes the pony lift its feet and prepares it for jumping. It also gives the rider an opportunity to practice their balance in the correct jumping position.

Your back should be straight.

It is essential that you wear a body protector when jumping.

Move your hands forward to allow the pony to stretch its neck forward.

Shorten the stirrups

For jumping, your stirrups should be about two holes shorter than usual. In the forward jumping position, you will find it easier to balance with shorter stirrups. You can adjust the stirrups once you are on the pony.

Learn to adjust a stirrup leather with one hand, keeping your foot in the stirrup.

Look for the next jump in the course as you land.

The pony tucks its front legs to clear the jump.

Brushing boots protect the pony's legs from knocks.

Your weight is in the stirrups, not on the pony's hindquarters.

The next jump

When the pony has landed, take up contact on the reins again and get ready for the next fence. If you are not balanced, you may pull on the reins, which can be painful and restrictive for the pony. If you are learning to jump, use a neckstrap at first to help you balance.

The pony lands on its forefeet, one after the other.

Cross-country

Wear a body protector when jumping.

Cross-country jumping is exciting and challenging. Competitions include hunter trials and a cross-country phase in one- and three-day events. Jumps are solid, and include ditches, logs, walls, stiles, and water jumps, which can be tricky. Some ponies are frightened to jump into water because they cannot see the bottom. They need confidence in their riders.

A DAY AT THE SHOW

COMPETING IN SHOWS is exciting for both rider and pony, and the more shows a rider goes to, the better they will become. There are many types of show, with classes for people and ponies of all levels. Riders can enter gymkhana games, showing classes, dressage, show jumping, or hunter trials. Although it is wonderful to win a prize, it is more important that both rider and pony enjoy themselves.

PREPARATION

A lot of preparation is needed before a show. Some things, such as cleaning tack and checking riding clothes, can be done before the actual day. Riders should plan their journey carefully, so they can arrive in plenty of time for their first event.

Grooming

For a special occasion such as a show, a pony should look its best. The mane and tail can be washed the day before and, if the weather is warm enough, you can give the pony a bath. Use shampoo with care, and avoid the eyes. Remove excess water with a sweat scraper, then walk the pony around until it is dry.

Transport

If a pony is traveling to the show in a trailer, it will need to wear traveling boots, which protect the legs from any knocks inside the trailer, and a tail bandage to stop the tail from rubbing. On arrival, the pony should be carefully led down the middle of the ramp.

Traveling boots

Quarter markings

1 Brush the coat on the hindquarters in the direction the hair lies with a damp brush.

2 Comb alternate squares of coat downward using a small comb.

3 When the quarter marks are completed, the pattern can be fixed with hairspray.

Getting ready

Once unloaded, the pony must be tied securely to the side of the trailer while you remove its boots and other traveling equipment. After the pony has settled, you can get dressed. Be careful not to dirty your clothes before the show!

Entering classes

Once the pony has relaxed after its journey, you can go and enter your classes. Even if you have entered them in advance, you must go and collect your number. Before the first class, put on the pony's tack and check that both you and your pony are looking neat and ready to enjoy yourselves.

Find out in advance what you are expected to wear for the events you are entering.

In dressage events, pony and rider perform special movements that test obedience.

Warming up

A pony will not perform well right from the trailer. If you are competing, you should arrive well before your first class so that you can warm up and focus your mind on the task ahead. Warming up involves stretching a pony's muscles and gently practicing moves. For example, in a jumping competition, this would involve a few practice jumps. Do not tire the pony out by charging around the ground with your friends.

To help the pony stay balanced, look for the next jump, rather than looking down.

Move your hands forward with the reins to give the pony's neck room to stretch out.

Rest your pony under the shade of a tree when the weather is warm, or with a blanket when it is chilly.

After the show

It is unfair to make the pony compete all day and expect it to perform well, so let it rest between classes with its saddle loosened off. Even if it doesn't win any prizes, always reward the pony well. Before you load it back into the trailer, give it some time to relax after all the excitement. Then take off its tack, sponge it down, and cover it with a sweat absorbing blanket, ready for the journey home.

Show jumping

In show jumping, competitors have to jump over a course of fences without the pony refusing, running out, or knocking down any of the fences.

RIDING SAFELY

RIDING A PONY is great fun, but it can be dangerous. If a rider is out alone, they should always let someone know where they are going, and when they expect to be back. It is a good idea to take some money to make a phone call, and a pocket first-aid kit, in case either the rider or the pony is injured. Only very experienced riders should ride on the road alone.

SAFETY ON THE ROAD

Before setting out, you should be confident that the pony's tack is in good condition. If the tack breaks when riding, it may cause an accident or make it difficult to control the pony. The best time to check the tack is when cleaning it. When riding on the road, you need to be alert at all times and must learn the correct hand signals and traffic regulations.

Wear sensible riding clothes with gloves and a riding hat.

Check girth
Before setting off, make sure that the girth is tight enough. Ponies often inflate their stomachs when a saddle is put on, so the girth cannot be done up properly. After a while their stomach shrinks again and the girth becomes too loose. Check the girth again a few minutes into the ride.

Tack should be in good condition and comfortable for the pony to wear.

Check shoes
A pony's shoes wear down quickly if the pony does a lot of road work. The shoes become smooth and have no grip, which makes the pony liable to slip. Check a pony's shoes regularly and arrange to have it reshod as often as necessary. The farrier may suggest a nonslip nail in two or more shoes. These are like ordinary nails, but have a small bump on the end, which helps the shoe grip the road. This is particularly useful when riding down hills.

Before riding, check that the pony's feet do not need picking out.

Hold the reins up off the ground while you inspect the pony's feet.

Road work can be hard on a pony's feet and legs, so never canter along the road.

Hold your arm out straight, so the signal is obvious.

Hand signals

Be especially vigilant in traffic, making sure that drivers know exactly where you are going by indicating in good time using clear hand signals. Ride on the same side as traffic and obey all road signs and traffic lights, in the same way as a driver would. If you meet a car in a narrow lane, go into a gateway or passing place as soon as possible, to allow the car to pass. Do not let the pony get so excited that it shies into the path of the car.

Shine boots prevent the pony cutting its leg with the other foot. They are fitted so that the straps are on the outside, and the protective face is on the inside.

Bell boots protect the heels.

Look carefully

Concentrate all the time when you are riding on the road. Even if there are no sounds of traffic, always check over your shoulder before turning left or right. Some cars are quiet and bicycles can be silent. Not all cyclists realize they can frighten a pony, and will not think to warn you when they are near. Keep to the side of the road so that cyclists and drivers can overtake. If you are riding in a group, stay together so it is easier for cars to pass.

Always give one last look over your shoulder before you turn.

If you are riding in single file, never overtake another rider unless the leader of the ride asks you to.

Never ride too close to any vehicle in case the driver starts the car, or opens the door unexpectedly.

Riding at night

If riding in the dark is unavoidable, take extra care to ensure that both you and the pony are as visible as possible. You can wear lights on the stirrups and fluorescent clothing, such as arm bands, a belt, or a sash. Ponies can also wear fluorescent clothing, such as an exercise sheet, leg bands, and strips that fit onto the bridle.

Safety at night is vital.

Fluorescent leg bands

Stirrup flashlight

Fluorescent belt

OUT AND ABOUT

BEFORE THE invention of the car, people who wanted to travel long distances did so on horseback, or in a horse-drawn carriage. Today, many people still ride horses and ponies for pleasure. Ponies like variety and love going out for a ride somewhere different, especially if they can have a good canter.

TRAIL RIDE

Once a rider is confident, they can go on a hack for an hour or two with other people from their riding school, or go out pony trekking for a day. Other activities include trail-riding holidays that involve traveling for several days, stopping overnight at different places where the ponies can stay too.

Trail riding in Iceland.

Keep to the marked path so that crops are not trampled.

Bridleways

Riding off the road, where you can often have a canter, is much nicer than riding in traffic. In some places, there are special paths that allow riders to ride across private land. Walkers sometimes use these paths too, so ride sensibly and be prepared in case your pony is startled by a pony or a dog.

Remember to shut the gate afterwards.

Opening a gate

Approach the gate and ask the pony to stand where you can reach the catch. Hold the reins in one hand and open the gate with the other. Try to hold on to the gate while you walk through, so it does not swing back and hit the pony. Hold the gate open for others to go through, too.

Don't forget to clean the tack after riding.

Attend to the pony's needs first.

End of the day

After a ride, take off the pony's tack, and make sure that the pony is comfortable. Brush the pony down, sponge off any sweat, and if necessary, put on a blanket, to stop it from catching a chill. Give the pony some water and hay, but do not give it hard feed immediately. A grass-fed pony may not need extra food, but do make sure that it has access to fresh water. Many ponies will enjoy a good roll after a long ride.

PONY BREEDS

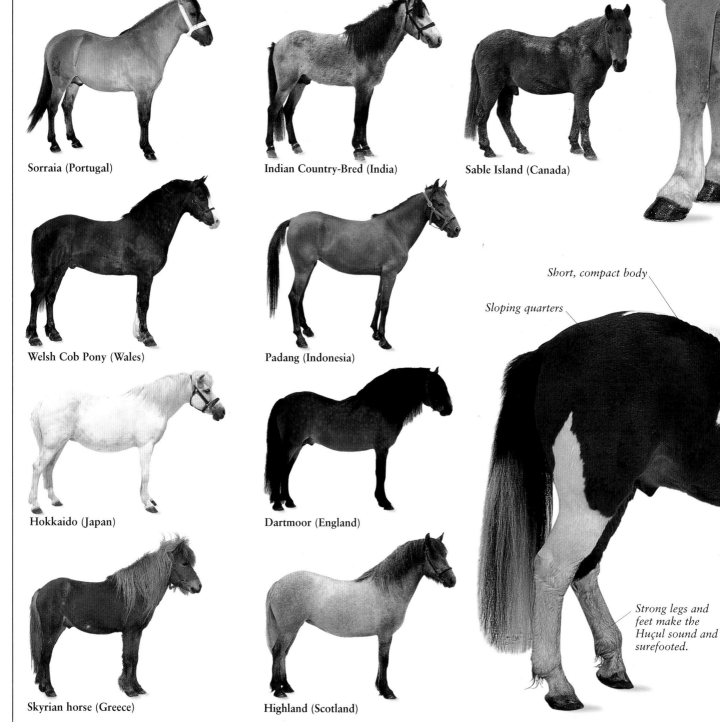

NATURAL PONY breeds evolved from groups of ponies living together. Their characteristics were determined by the conditions in which they lived. Those that lived in a harsh climate with little food were small, hardy animals; those that lived in mountains and rough terrain were surefooted.

BREEDS

Humans have developed new pony breeds all over the world. Each breed has recognized characteristics, such as size and conformation. The pedigrees of accepted ponies are recorded in an official stud book.

Sorraia (Portugal)

Indian Country-Bred (India)

Sable Island (Canada)

Welsh Cob Pony (Wales)

Padang (Indonesia)

Hokkaido (Japan)

Dartmoor (England)

Skyrian horse (Greece)

Highland (Scotland)

Short, compact body

Sloping quarters

Strong legs and feet make the Huçul sound and surefooted.

Haflinger

The Haflinger is a strong, hardy breed that can live for more than 40 years. Ponies of this breed are naturally surefooted, with excellent limbs and feet. The Haflinger is chestnut or palomino, with a flaxen mane and tail.

Medium-sized head

Huçul

The Huçul of Poland is a breed of pony used as a workhorse on farms in southern Poland and also as a pack horse.

Sandalwood (Indonesia)

Galiceno (Mexico)

Caspian (Arabian peninsular)

Connemara (Ireland)

Pottock (France)

Shetland (Scotland)

Ariegeois (France)

Sumba (Indonesia)

Hackney Pony

Java (Indonesia)

New Forest Pony (England)

59

Glossary

Aids The signals that a rider uses to communicate with a pony, such as the hands, legs, and voice.

Bit A piece of tack attached to the reins that goes in a pony's mouth.

Breed A group of horses or ponies (or other animal) that share the same characteristics and passes these down to their offspring, e.g. Thoroughbred, Welsh Pony, Dartmoor Pony.

Cast A pony becomes cast when it lies down or rolls in a confined space, and is unable to get up again because it is stuck.

Cavesson noseband The simplest type of noseband. A cavesson is also a type of headgear. It has a ring on the noseband to which a lunge line can be attached.

Changing the rein Changing the direction in which you ride around an arena.

Colt A young male pony or horse.

Concentrates Food, such as oats, coarse mix, or barley, which in small amounts contains high levels of energy.

Conformation The shape of a pony and the way it is made.

Cross-country A sport in which rider and pony jump around a course of rustic jumps set across country.

Dandy brush A medium-hard brush with long bristles for removing mud from a pony's coat.

Dock The bony part at the top of a pony's tail.

Dressage A sport in which rider and pony are judged for their performance of a series of special movements around an arena.

Eventing A sport in which rider and pony have to do dressage, cross-country, and showjumping.

Farrier A person trained to look after a pony's feet and to put on shoes.

Filly A young female pony or horse.

Flehmen When a pony curls its lip in response to an unusual smell or taste.

Foal A pony or horse up to 12 months old.

Frog The tough, elastic material in the center of a pony's sole, under the foot.

Gait The way in which a pony moves its legs. The four main gaits are walk, trot, canter, and gallop.

Gamgee Cotton wool covered in gauze, which is used under a bandage for padding.

Gelding A male horse or pony that can no longer reproduce.

Girth A strap placed around a pony's belly to keep the saddle in place.

Grooming Brushing a pony's coat to keep its skin clean, shiny, and healthy and to make the pony more comfortable.

Gymkhana A show in which riders and ponies take part in mounted games.

Hands The traditional unit of measurement in which the height of horses and ponies is described. One hand equals about 4 inches (10 cm), which is roughly the width of an adult hand.

Hindquarters The back end of a pony, including the hind (back) legs.

Inside The side of the rider and pony on the inside when riding in a circle.

Leg up The action of someone helping a rider to spring into the saddle by lifting them up by the leg.

Lunging When a pony is schooled in circles on a lunging line by someone on the ground.

Mare A female horse or pony.

Near side The left-hand side of a pony, looking from back to front.

Off side The right-hand side of a pony, looking from back to front.

Outside The side of the rider and pony on the outside when riding in a circle.

Pace The speed at which a pony moves.

Pony A horse that is no more than 14.2 hands high (1.47 m).

Quick-release knot A knot that is secure, but can be undone quickly.

Roughage Plant material, such as hay, grass, or chaff, which makes up the major part of a pony's diet.

Showjumping A sport in which a rider and pony jump a course of jumps, usually colored, in an arena.

Stallion A male horse or pony that is used for breeding.

Tack A general term for the saddle, bridle, and other equipment needed to ride a pony.

Transition A change of gait up or down, for example, from a walk to a trot or from a canter to a trot.

Type A group of ponies that are a similar shape, but do not pass the characteristics to their offspring, e.g. riding pony or cob.

Index

Useful addresses

American Horse Council
1700 K Street NW
Suite 30
Washington, DC
20006

American Horse Protection
Association
1000 29th Street
T-100 Washington, DC
20007

American Horse Shows
Association
220 E. 42nd Street
#409
New York, NY
10017

American Riding Instructor
Certificate Program
PO Box 282

The International League for the
Protection of Horses
Anne Colvin House
Snetterton
Norfolk
England

North American Riding for the
Handicapped Association
PO Box 33150
Denver, CO
80233

Acknowledgments

DK would like to thank the following people for their help in the production of this book:

The models, Mary Sharman, Tash Seeley, Ann Marie Barker, Kelly Butler, Sophie Thomas, Eric Lin, and Zoe Ingram. Netty Seeley and Pamy Hutton and everyone at Tallands Riding School who gave us such good advice.
Linda Gardner, Sally and David Waters for all their support and help.

Picture credits
The publisher would like to thank the following for their kind permission to reproduce their photographs:

Key: l=left, r=right, t=top, c=center, a=above, b=below

Animal Photography: 19c; **Bruce Coleman Limited:** William S. Paton 14ca; Hans Reinhard 21cb; **Robert Harding Picture Library:** M. Black 9br; **Image Bank:** Patrick Fagot 14tl; **Impact Photos:** Paul O'Driscoll 15cr; **Frank Lane Picture Agency:** David Hosking 25bc; Mark Newman 15tc; Silvestris 15cra; W. Wisniewski 10bl, 54cl; **Bob Langrish:** 16cl, 18cr, 34–35c, 51bl, 53bl, 58–59; **Daphne Steinberg** 57clb; **Only Horses:** 14–15c, 14bl, 18tl, 18cl, 30–31c; **Oxford Scientific Films:** David Curl 15br; **Frank Spooner Pictures:** E. Sander/Liaison 20br; **Tony Stone Images:** J. F. Preedy 21cl.